SMART GUIDE TO STOP USING STUPID WORDS!

30-Minute Ride to a Successful, Peaceful Mind

ANDREW KAPUR

SMART GUIDE TO STOP USING STUPID WORDS!
30-Minute Ride to a Successful, Peaceful Mind

Copyright © 2018 by ANDREW KAPUR

All Rights Reserved.

No part of this publication may be reproduced in any form or by any means, including photocopying, scanning, recording, or otherwise without prior written permission of the copyright holder, Andrew Kapur.

ISBN: 978-1-9994726-0-3

Table of Contents

INTRODUCTION	7
Chapter 1: Why We Use So Many Effing Negative Words	9
Chapter 2: Love, Fear, and Oreo Cookies	13
Chapter 3: Thinking in Pictures and Drinking Pitchers	17
Chapter 4: Words to Stop Using Right Now and Forever	21
Chapter 5: Affirmations and Living Past Your 245th Birthday	27
Chapter 6: The Reason That Everyone (Including You!) Should Avoid Passing Judgement	31
Chapter 7: Free Mega-List of Secret Words	36
Chapter 8: The Three Most Useful Words (For Real) and Pac Man	39
CONCLUSION	43

"This is a valuable book for anyone who wants to improve their lives. It is as compelling as it funny. Finally, I have a book that I can actually finish."

Faisal Butt

Comedian, Just for Laughs (Montreal/Toronto), Serious XM winner of the Top Comic Competition

Dedication

My Family

My mom has always encouraged me to pursue my dreams and follow my heart. She is also my first editor and accountability buddy. My father taught me to compare myself to the best and forget the rest. My brother has set a high bar for success and is a role model for me—whom I constantly strive to outperform.

My Friends

To all the people who help me every day reach higher and succeed! A very special thanks to Kate F, Rabbiya A, Bruno C, Emanuela B, and Faisal B.

GOD

Introduction

To state that our use of language is flawed is an understatement. The reality is that our use, or rather misuse, of words is super f*cked up. There are so many beautiful words that are useful and necessary to express our thoughts. However, there are also a great deal of negative words that are useless, should be avoided, and actually cause us harm. Unfortunately, most people are completely unaware of this fact and use a lexicon of destructive words daily. This is not their fault, nor is it yours. After reading this book, you will develop a new appreciation for words which will, in turn, significantly improve your relationships, career, life, high score in Pac-Man, and much more!

The format of this book is light and fun while providing you, the reader, with many useful tools that you may start using immediately. In this book you will learn why we mistakenly choose negative words over positive ones, the two emotions that motivate every decision, our process of thinking in pictures, which words to stop using right now, positive affirmations, the reason to avoid judging people, secret marketing words, and, most importantly, the three most useful and powerful words to start using and focusing on every day.

CHAPTER 1

Why We Use So Many Effing Negative Words

CHAPTER 1: WHY WE USE SO MANY EFFING NEGATIVE WORDS

Robert Schrauf conducted a study which revealed that negative words dominate our vocabulary. Would you believe that his research shows that our proportions of words are 50 percent negative, 30 percent positive and 20 percent neutral? Reflect on this fact for a minute. Half of everything you say and think is tied to a negative emotion. Across thirty-seven different languages, seven words to describe emotions were discovered that have very similar meanings. These words are joy (or happiness), fear, anger, sadness, disgust, shame, and guilt.[1] To state it another way for all you math geniuses, the ratio is one out of seven words are positive, or 85.7% of the words are negative. That is just a sad fact that makes me angry, as well as fills me with shame, guilt, and disgust for the human race (oh sh*t, now I'm doing it too).

The reason that vocabulary is so heavily weighted to the negative side is a flaw in our DNA from old obsolete programs that still run in our mind. Think of cavemen times. The emotion of fear would trigger a mental response that indicated a threat to our life or basic survival. The signal that our brains received can roughly translate to: "Run away now, as fast as you can, or fight to the death." For this reason, fear received all of our attention and needed to be addressed immediately. This led to the brain focusing more attention on negative emotions than on positive ones. Joy, on the other hand, required little mental focus. This, in turn, hardwired our brains to favor negative emotions and words over positive ones. The same outdated programs are the reason humans see more shades of green than any other color. This ability comes from a time when primitive humans began consuming fruits and leaves from flowering plants while mostly living in forests or jungles. Another reason was to avoid predators (some of you already know this fact from watching the awesome television mini-series "Fargo").

According to Simon T. Bailey, by the time a child reaches the age of 17, they have heard the word "No" 150,000 times. This is compared to hearing "Yes" only 5,000 times. The more you hear the word "No" and, in turn, let others reinforce all the things you can't do, the worse it is for your mentality. Neurological pathways are created in the brain that cause you to limit your creativity and inborn genius. This leads you to give up on trying new things and prevents you from even beginning to conceive of them.

Now that you are armed with this knowledge, the next time someone tells you that you cannot achieve your goal, that you are not smart enough, or simply that your idea will not work, calmly tell them to please f*ck off. Then proceed by internally affirming that you can achieve whatever you put your mind to. There are, of course, some exceptions to every rule. If you are over the age of 60 and want to begin a career as a professional sports athlete, you should probably reconsider your focus. We will explore affirmations in more detail in Chapter 5 to help reprogram your brain to a more positive mind frame.

There is an old sales trick that instructs salespeople to ask customers three questions where the answer will be a resounding yes. After responding affirmatively three times, the brain is stuck in a positive track and more likely to respond with a "Yes" answer for the fourth question (you can try this with your significant other the next time you want them to…). This works in a similar way when we are conditioned to a negative response.

Think of the last time you walked into a clothing store and a staff member asked you if you needed any help. Most people respond with an answer that begins with the word "No". This is true even if they actually do need help, and they often will ask for assistance at a later time. We are programmed into this negative frame of mind. For the next few days, try saying "Yes" as much as possible in every situation and see what happens. Be aware of how it makes you feel (note that you should still say no to drugs, and there will be some other exceptions as well).

Chapter 2

Love, Fear and Oreo cookies

CHAPTER 2: LOVE, FEAR, AND OREO COOKIES

Have you ever thought to yourself, "What really motivates me to do the things I do?" There are two primal emotions that push us towards taking action. These emotions are *love* and *fear*. Every choice can be traced back to fit into one of these two categories. Think of them as the roots of the decision-making process.

According to Captain Obvious, the emotion of love is positive and the emotion of fear is negative. It should be noted that the majority of the time, a love-based decision is correct and a fear-based one is incorrect. You should start your decision process based on love. There are really only two situations where fear is helpful. The first scenario involves you facing a life or death situation—like being chased by a bear, a wild pack of wolves, or zombies. Fear is, of course, also useful to keep us from taking unnecessary risks and making outright wrong decisions. Some examples of fear protecting us include stopping us from walking blindly into traffic, insulting a stranger that is twice our size, eating Meecrob, touching a hot stove, or having a gasoline fight with our friends.

I would like you to think of each emotion as having a large spectrum of intensity. Love, in the deepest sense, is the strongest word in the English language to express the extreme feeling of liking someone. To clarify, think of the phrase "I am madly in love with you." One big intensity step below this would be to say, "I am fond of you." The opposite end of the spectrum would be to say, "I tolerate you." Just imagine the reaction you would get by looking into your significant other's eyes over a candlelit dinner and saying, "I tolerate you." In general, people tend to misuse the word love. In my opinion, it is improper to say, "I love Oreo cookies" (even though they are super yummy). A better choice of words would be to state, "I like Oreo cookies." In Chapter 4, we will look deeper into the reasons why we should be aware of the words we use and the intensity to produce the desired results. Fear, as discussed in Chapter 1, is the most powerfully engrained emotion in our biology for the purpose of survival. The spectrum of intensity goes from feeling slightly apprehensive to being in an outright state of terror (like when you see a scary clown).

Here are some compelling reasons to make decisions based on love. According to an article co-written by Gary Wilson and Marnia Robinson entitled "Love and Fear"[2], when we feel love, our brain releases the chemical oxytocin. Fear increases the stress hormones adrenaline and cortisol. Adrenaline is helpful when produced in short time intervals and used up quickly. If too much of it is produced and not used up by the body, it turns into a poison and is unhealthy. Cortisol has a number of negative side effects including breaking down muscles, bones, and joints, as well as causing our immune system to be less effective and increasing our chances of heart disease, high blood pressure, obesity, diabetes, and osteoporosis. Oxytocin induces emotional bonding as well as producing the opposite effects of cortisol by healing the body. Our friendly chemical oxytocin is also responsible for tricking us into experiencing the amazing feeling of falling in love when we are in a romantic relationship (if you didn't already know this, then you might be feeling right now like you did as a child when you found out Santa Claus and the Tooth-fairy are not real. My apologies!).

When beginning to form any decision, determine for yourself what the root emotion is. Are you making this choice based on fear or out of love? Do you get up and go to work because you like your job, or because you fear not paying your rent, mortgage, or bills? Start by being aware of your root motivating emotion. Then reflect to see if any fear-based decisions can be reframed or restated into love-based ones.

It helps to have a positive frame of mind when you wake up in the morning. Unfortunately, sometimes this state of mind can be derailed during the course of the day. I remember waking up one day and getting ready for work. I was very happy when I awoke—ready to conquer the day. Within the first fifteen minutes, I had spilled hot coffee on my lap (reproductive organs), experienced a shaving mishap which left me with half an eyebrow, and dropped my toothbrush in the toilet. I decided to cancel work and go back to bed.

CHAPTER 3

Thinking in Pictures and Drinking Pitchers

CHAPTER 3: THINKING IN PICTURES AND DRINKING PITCHERS

Remember that we all think in pictures. We then proceed to translate those mental images, often crudely, into words.

Let's start with a simple example that you are probably familiar with. I will tell you, "Don't think of a monkey riding a tricycle." What did you just do? You thought of a monkey riding a tricycle. It is impossible not to think of a monkey riding a tricycle because you need to register in your mind what it is exactly you are not supposed to think of before you attempt to do so. This is a harmless example, but some mental images can be quite destructive. What do you think of when you read the words "Hot Sex"? Did you picture two three-letter words? I didn't think so.

Plato, the great Greek philosopher, wrote about this a long time ago. If I ask you to think of a horse, you understand what specific animal I'm writing about and the animal I am asking you to picture in your mind. Is the horse in your imagination big or small? Which color is the horse? Does it have a saddle or is it wild? The point is that somewhere in our collective imagination, we all understand the meaning of the word "horse", yet our mental images all differ. The conclusion is that there exists an archetypal horse that fits all our imagined pictures (honestly, tell me that you never smoked a joint or drank three or more pitchers of beer and thought of this scenario).

I will now ask you to think of a lemon. I want you to picture the lemon in your left hand. Think of the color, feel the yellow skin in your palm. Now imagine you put the lemon on a cutting board and use a knife to cut it into two pieces. Picture taking one half of the lemon and bring it under your nose. Smell the lemony freshness. Take a few seconds to really visualize it in your mind. Now take a big bite! If you did the exercise correctly, your mouth produced extra saliva to account for the sourness of the lemon. Since you have read and are now familiar with the instructions on how to do the visualization exercise, you can retry it with your eyes closed, which will be much more effective. This is a common experiment to prove that your mind does not really know reality from your imagined world. (You can retry the same experiment using a piece of dog poop instead of a lemon, but I don't recommend it).

We can use this natural process of thinking in pictures to our advantage. I would recommend making yourself a vision board to help your mind focus on the objects, emotions, and experiences you desire. The process is super simple. You can start by deciding what you want to manifest in your life. Then you find pictures of those things and cut them out of a magazine or print them from a computer. These pictures could include your favourite luxury car, your dream house, Pee Wee's Playhouse, a vacation spot, or inspiring quotes and positive words. Take the pictures and tape or glue them to a board.

Place the vision board somewhere that it will be seen every day. That's it! Please send me pictures of your vision boards along with your success stories to *info@AndrewKapur.com.*

CHAPTER 4

Words to Stop Using Right Now and Forever

CHAPTER 4: WORDS TO STOP USING RIGHT NOW AND FOREVER

I would like you to please sit up straight, log off Facebook, pause that YouTube video, stop texting, and mute the television. This sh*t is about to get real.

There is a list of words that should be eliminated entirely from our vocabulary. I have personally done so years ago. I decided to create this book because I hear these harmful words used every day on YouTube videos, webinars, and on television. This does not mean that there are subjects we can no longer discuss due to limitations on the words we allow ourselves to use. Instead, we should choose to negate positive words, rather than use negative ones that require us to imagine undesirable images.

The Oxford English Dictionary contains full entries for 171,476 words in current use and 47,156 obsolete words (2013). Obsolete is used to indicate that a word is no longer in active use in speech and writing. I was compelled to search for words that have been removed from the dictionary. The word "snout-fair" was removed. Can you guess what it means? It means handsome or to have a good looking face. This word will not be missed by anyone, ever.

Most native English speakers know about 25,000 to 30,000 words. What I find interesting is that 3000 words cover about 95% of everything you read or hear on television. Thousands of new words are added every year. You can Google search "new words list January 2018" if you are really interested in the latest words to be added. (You will be happy to know that the adjective "dickish" was added in 2018. It's about time! The definition is exactly what you think it is). These statistics lead me to believe that we could comfortably cut out lots of negative words with little to no consequence in our overall communication.

The best example I can give you is the word that bothers me the most. It is the word "sick". This is a destructive and horrible word. I prefer to use the words "not healthy" instead. This way I have to picture health, which has a positive effect, instead of "s*ck", which creates a negative picture in my head (please note that the word "f*ck" is much less offensive to me). It is however okay to use the word sick when describing an awesome experience. An example of this would be, "That was an amazing concert. The guitarist is sick!". The reason being that this does not produce the same negative mental image.

We should also not use health issue symptoms as nouns, but rather as verbs. Instead of saying, "I have a cold," we should say, "I am colding." This tells our brain that it is a temporary state that we are in that will pass.

CHAPTER 4: WORDS TO STOP USING RIGHT NOW AND FOREVER

Example List of Words to Stop Using and Better Alternatives

BAD   GOOD

Sick   Unhealthy, not healthy

Angry   Not feeling calm

Stressed   Not feeling able to cope

Violent   Not peaceful

A complete list of negative words can be found at this website *http://positivewordsresearch.com/list-of-negative-words/* and a list of positive words can be found at *http://positivewordsresearch.com/list-of-positive-words/*. Some examples of negative words that I like are "unsuccessful", "unwise", and "unfriendly".

To really drive home this concept, let's take some advice from someone really amazing. Here is a great quote from Mother Teresa: "I was once asked why I don't participate in anti-war demonstrations. I said that I will never do that, but as soon as you have a pro-peace rally, I'll be there." Take a moment to let the wisdom of those words really sink into your mind.

It is also important to try and avoid extreme words as well, or at least be conscious of when you are using them. For example, instead of saying, "I hate this," you can say, "I dislike this." This will not only make you a more eloquent speaker but will also allow you to access extreme words when absolutely necessary thereby guaranteeing a strong impact on the intended listener. If someone uses extreme words often, those words will lose their strength. This is the same for swear words.

If a habitually calm and polite person (think of the kindest, most softly spoken person you ever met) suddenly raises their voice and yells at someone to shut the f*ck up, it will be felt with force. On the other hand, if someone swears constantly, the impact of the swear words will lose all meaning.

CHAPTER 5

Affirmations and Living Past Your 245th Birthday

CHAPTER 5: AFFIRMATIONS AND LIVING PAST YOUR 245TH BIRTHDAY

Our thoughts create our beliefs. Our beliefs combined with emotion create our reality. Think in terms of computer code. Why would you insert words into your mental program that hurt you? This is the opposite of the intention of affirmations. Positive affirmations are powerful and used by people to permeate their subconscious with positive reinforcement.

Please remember that affirmations should always be in the present tense and be coined to reflect your ideal outcome. One of my favourite affirmations is, "Every day in every way, everything is getting better and better." Another powerful statement is, "My subconscious mind is my partner in success." Both of these affirmations come for John Kehoe's book "Mind Power"[3]. Here is one last affirmation that is fun and produces unpredictable realities: "Lucky surprises." Feel free to incorporate these in your everyday life. ***(subscribe to my website at *www.andrewkapur.com* to get your free copy of my personal affirmation list that led to my #1 Billboard hit and successful music career).

It should be obvious by now but just to be sure, I remind you to never use negative words in your affirmations or state them in a way that negates a negative. Here is an example to clarify: "I never lose." This is a bad affirmation and what your mind will reinforce is "I lose" (please re-read the monkey on a tricycle example from chapter 3 if you need further clarification).

You may also want to create three-word mantras to use depending on the day, situation, and event taking place. My most frequently used mantra is "Fun, relaxed, and organized" (coined by John Kehoe originally as "Organized, relaxed, and fun")[3]. This works well for almost every occasion and can be used daily. Try coming up with some yourself. Sometimes people like to make the three words an acronym, which can make it easier to recall (FRO: fun, relaxed, organized doesn't really work so well).

In the movie "Kiss of Death", Nicholas Cage's character, Little Junior Brown, states, "I have an acronym for myself. Know what it is? B.A.D. B.A.D... Balls, Attitude, Direction. You should give yourself an acronym... 'cause it helps you visualize your goals." Then David Caruso's character, Jimmy Kilmartin, responds, "How about F.A.B.? Fucked At Birth." Little Junior Brown responds, "No good. Too negative."[4]

Be conscious of your inner dialog as well as any statements you make about yourself. You are constantly feeding your mind information that it is processing and using to create your inner belief systems. Recently I was at lunch with a very close friend of mine who works two jobs. He stated openly to myself and two other friends the following: "I work too many hours. I will probably be dead within 10 years." I was, of course, horrified by this negative statement! I immediately addressed the issue and demanded that he never repeat it again. I asked him to replace this ridiculous statement in his mind with a quote from the movie "Talladega Nights." Ricky Bobby said, "No one lives forever, no one. But with advances in modern science and my high-level income, it's not crazy to think I can live to be 245, maybe 300."[5]

Chapter 6

The Reason That Everyone (Including You!) Should Avoid Passing Judgment

CHAPTER 6: THE REASON THAT EVERYONE (INCLUDING YOU!) SHOULD AVOID PASSING JUDGEMENT

The power of words can lift someone up or hurt someone deeply depending on which words we choose to use. Sometimes we are unaware of how painful a simple insult can be to someone. Other times we could give someone a seemingly meaningless compliment and it lifts their spirits beyond what we could have imagined. Please choose your words wisely (you wonderful, smart, awesome, beautiful person).

Now that we are aware of that, let me share with you another reason why you should not insult people. Insults can do more harm to the person delivering the insult than the person receiving it. This is again due to the way our brain is wired. When we make a statement in our mind or out loud about a person, our brain interprets it as if we are thinking or speaking about ourselves. To clarify, you think to yourself, "Oh wow, he is really stupid" and your mind registers it as, "Oh wow, I am really stupid." This will lead your subconscious to steer you towards making stupid decisions to validate the statement. To reinforce what was discussed earlier, you should always internally think of a person, at the least, as not smart. You should eliminate the use of the word stupid altogether (yes I am aware of the irony of this book's title).

I always look for the best qualities in people. Sometimes you meet someone who qualifies as your definition of stupid and you can't help thinking it. When this happens to me, I usually start doing some positive affirmations to neutralize the negative thought I just experienced. In time, you can get your own mind to be accustomed to not passing judgment on people.

Chapter 7
Free Mega-List of Secret Words

CHAPTER 7: FREE MEGA-LIST OF SECRET WORDS

I can remember reading a compilation of words that were listed as the most useful in advertising. These words can be most often found on the cover of women's magazines or in online ads. I'm confident that you are familiar with them, but I will give you a short list to illustrate my point. These words include but are not limited to "free", "fun", "secret", "guaranteed", "new", "proven", and "instant". Have you ever seen a magazine cover that read "Inside we reveal the three secrets that are guaranteed to make you lose weight instantly"?

Then there are words that really have no meaning at all but seem to somehow hold pseudo power. These words are "mega", "ultra", "super", and "hyper". The reason I share these words with you is to make you aware of how they influence you, and how they influence others. This is another example of the power of words. So the next time you see some dish soap that promises to leave your plates and glasses ultra clean, take notice and think to yourself, "What the f*ck is the difference between ultra clean and just plain clean?"

Another way that we get influenced is by the use of framing. Please allow me to explain. The most basic example to illustrate the meaning of framing is by answering the following question: Is the glass half empty or half full? Framing goes well beyond this question and often unconsciously impacts our decisions.

Suppose you see a product that is labelled as "90% effective". This seems very efficient. If the same product was labelled

"10% of the time it doesn't work," you might not be inclined to purchase it. Both statements express the same result, but one is positive and the other negative. Maybe you read a label for fruit juice that reads "Made with 80% real fruit juice." What if it read "Made with only 20% chemicals?" Would you still want to drink it?

Real estate agents will present a small home as being "cozy". They will never say the word "small" because in this context the word seems negative or undesirable. Euphemisms are words that replace harsher and more unpleasant words. You might have heard the term "adult entertainment". This sounds much better than "pornography". Another example is the common saying "slept together" instead of "had sex." Euphemisms are effective because we think in pictures and our brain does not take the time to process the inverse or negative side of the same statement. Be on the lookout for framing in advertisements and also, most importantly, in your own inner dialog when making decisions.

CHAPTER 8

The Three Most Useful Words (For Real) and Pac-Man

CHAPTER 8: THE THREE MOST USEFUL WORDS (FOR REAL) AND PAC MAN

Let's close this off on a positive note, with the three most important and powerful words in the English language. (First, kindly close your eyes and take three slow deep breaths, inhaling through your nose and exhaling through your mouth. Do you feel calmer and more focused? Great!). These words are "gratitude", "forgiveness", and "love". Wait! Before you stop reading because you think this book has just taken a really hippy, sappy, and odd turn, please allow me to explain.

Focusing your mind on gratitude will bring more experiences and events into your life to be grateful for. When you acknowledge good fortune with gratitude, your subconscious mind gets programmed to create more of the same feeling. This gratitude can be directed towards God or the universe. Every time something good comes into your life, be sure to take a moment to inwardly say thanks. The more you say thank you, the more things you will have to be thankful for.

It is irrelevant how big or small the pleasant event you experience is—just be grateful. The next time you get fast food from a drive-in and they don't mess up your order, be thankful!

Forgiveness is sometimes a challenge for many people. The act of forgiveness can be separated into two divisions. The first one involves forgiving others and the second one involves forgiving yourself. You absolutely need to find a way to forgive both yourself and others. The data collected by the superman and founder of Mind Valley, Vishen Lakhiani, shows us definitively why it is so important. (Check out the complete article at *https://blog.mindvalley.com/studying-brain-with-meditation/*). A study was done on the brain patterns of highly spiritual Zen masters who have meditated for 21-40 years. The main difference between their advanced peaceful minds and the average person's mind was forgiveness. If you want to be really happy and obtain inner peace, you must learn to forgive. There is no other way. (I realize that took a really deep turn. I bet you didn't see that coming! To lighten the mood, do you remember that part in the movie "Training Day" where Denzel says, "King Kong ain't got sh*t on me!"[6] That was an awesome scene).

Gratitude and forgiveness lead to love. Forgiving yourself leads to loving yourself. Loving yourself allows you to love others and in turn receive love at a deeper and more meaningful level. Gratitude to a higher power reduces your stress, lowers the negative part of your ego-self, and lets love into your life.

Now I would like to share, as promised, a quick strategy for Pac-Man. Turning corners is faster for Pac-Man than the ghosts chasing you. Avoid the spot below the ghost hut as best you can. Through artificial intelligence, (AI) the ghosts are not programmed to chase you; they only move in set patterns relative to your Pac-Man character. That is all for now!

Conclusion

Congratulations on reading this far. We are almost done. One last powerful, ultra, mega important, secret section to go. Thanks for taking the time to read this guidebook. I hope that you've enjoyed it and that it has provided you with some useful information that inspires you to re-evaluate the vocabulary that you use daily. If you are interested in diving deeper into what you have just read, my in-depth, complete online course, "Smart Guide to Stop Using Stupid Words!" will be available soon! Last, but not least, please keep a look out for my next book, "Note to Higher Self", where I turn your love for music into practical tools to benefit your life. Check out my website at **_www.AndrewKapur.com_** for updates.

I leave you with these final words. Now that you have a better understanding of your vocabulary—its power, which words to avoid, which ones to focus on and which ones are meaningless—what will you choose to do with the knowledge? Remember, knowledge is not power unless it is used. After really analyzing and understanding our language and the use of it, I like to reflect on the beauty of silence. Please note that silence is often more powerful than any words. Our ego-self can benefit from silence, but our soul was made to sing.

CONCLUSION

Here is one last piece of advice: replace "Sorry" with "Thank you." Instead of, "Sorry I'm late," try saying, "Thank you for waiting on me." Another example could be instead of saying "Sorry I'm drunk and high," you could say,"…"

References

1. ABCnews.com

    Article Author: Lee Dye

    Study: Negative Words Dominate Language

    Why Do Humans Have More Words to Describe the Negative?

    Feb. 2, 2005 —

    Interview with Robert Schrauf

2. http://www.entelechyjournal.com/robinsonwilson.htm

    Article Author: Gary Wilson and Marnia Robinson

    Study: Love and Fear

    Copyright © 2006   Entelechy: Mind & Culture. New Paltz, NY. All rights reserved

3. Author: John Kehoe

    Book: Mind Power

    Published by Zoetic Inc. (1987)

4. Movie: Kiss of Death (1995) film

    Directed by Barbet Schroeder

    Distributed by: 20th Century Fox

    Reference: https://www.imdb.com/title/tt0113552/quotes

REFERENCES

5. Movie: Talladega Nights: The Ballad of Ricky Bobby (2006) film

> *Directed by Adam McKay. Written by Adam McKay and Will Ferrell.*
>
> *Distributed by: Columbia Pictures*
>
> *Reference: https://en.wikiquote.org/wiki/Talladega_Nights:_The_Ballad_of_Ricky_Bobby*

6. Movie: Training Day (2001) film

> *Directed by Antoine Fuqua. Written by David Ayer*
>
> *Distributed by: Warner Bros. Pictures*
>
> *Reference: https://www.imdb.com/title/tt0139654/quotes*

Notes

Help!
Action Required!
Please and Thank You

I really appreciate you reading my book. If you would like to share any comments with me, please send them to *info@AndrewKapur.com.*

I need your help to continue writing helpful, informative, and fun books.

Please write me a helpful review and comment with your thoughts about this book on the Amazon website.

I thank you in advance for being awesome!

-**Andrew Kapur**

Made in the USA
Lexington, KY
07 February 2019